# PERFECT PRUNING

Simon Akeroyd

National Trust

First published in the United Kingdom in 2019 by
National Trust Books
43 Great Ormond Street
London
WC1N 3HZ

An imprint of Pavilion Books Company Ltd

ISBN 978-1-91135-871-8

A CIP catalogue record for this book is available from the British Library.

10  9  8  7  6  5  4  3  2  1

Reproduction by Mission Productions Ltd, Hong Kong
Printed and bound by 1010 Printing International Ltd, China

This book can be ordered direct from the publisher at www.pavilionbooks.com

Interior illustrations by Abi Read

# CONTENTS

# INTRODUCTION

Plants do perfectly well outside our gardens without our intervention. So why we spend so much time worrying about pruning is a mystery. The wild looks beautiful as it is, so much so that one of the key modern gardening trends is naturalism. Yet we all seem to need advice when it comes to pruning in our own gardens, some sense that there is a perfect formula for keeping them healthy, pretty and productive. There is a cherished belief, which is hard to dismiss, that as long we follow the correct rules we won't accidentally damage, or worse, kill our favourite plant or create something so ugly that neighbours will snigger and point at it as they look over the garden fence.

There is no doubt that professional gardeners have occasionally played upon these fears. What should be helpful advice is too often high-handedly delivered as a prescription. Yet pruning is one of the oldest plant interventions around. Pictures on the walls of Egyptian monuments show pharaohs gifting pruned trees in pots to the gods over four thousand years ago. So, how hard can it be?

The pioneers of pruning techniques were working from close observation and instinct, not from a book of rules. Mother Nature herself has her own methods of pruning, with animals cropping off low branches to create clear trunks on trees or nibbling the young, tasty growth of shrubs. This would have given early gardeners an understanding that plants could withstand a certain amount of chopping back but perhaps not too much. They would have noticed that there were more apples on the horizontal branches of an apple tree than on the upright ones, and tried to encourage this. They practised tree pruning to produce more firewood and straighter wood for building long before the techniques of coppicing for coloured stems and canopy-raising crept into the garden.

So why worry too much? A little understanding of how plants grow, some common sense, the right tools and off you go.

In the garden the amount of pruning you want or need to do depends largely on your philosophy and personality. For some people gardening is a conversation between two living things. All pruning involves wounding plants, and so minimal intervention is the name of the game. You might only wish to prune as a kind of 'medical' intervention, removing diseased limbs and stems, but otherwise leaving the plant pretty much alone. If this is the way you want to manage your garden it makes sense to try to provide the right environment in the first place. Make sure that you have the right plants in the right place and that they have the right amount of space to grow. Choose plants that suit your garden conditions as this will reduce the need for human intervention – happy, healthy plants mean less dead and diseased wood. Water and fertilise sensibly, and at the right time, to prevent more growth than would be natural.

Most of us, though, prefer to take a little more control in our gardens and, if we are being honest, our needs usually outweigh the needs of the plants we grow. We want healthy plants but also to tip the natural balance between growth, flowers and fruit in one direction or another. We like our apple trees to produce as much fruit as possible, for example, but our hedges to be leafy and dense. We want our climbers to cover the ugly shed roof but not to clamber all over the wall behind. For some people every shrub and tree in their garden must be neat and tidy, with not a leaf or stem out of place.

Ultimately pruning is about bending plant growth to our will; manipulating, cajoling and occasionally downright bullying plants, but that just makes the whole process more interesting. By the end of this book you should have all the confidence and tools you need to take up the challenge, as gently or as forcefully as you want.

# BASICS

# REASONS FOR PRUNING

There are a whole host of reasons for pruning. Most people have no problem understanding the importance of removing the dead, diseased or damaged parts of a shrub or tree. Pruning is the easiest way to control infections or pest attacks in their early stages without having to resort to harmful chemicals, while being aware that the torn wounds where branches have been damaged can often themselves be entry points for further problems. As damage is very often caused by two branches rubbing together, pruning out crossing branches is usually done at the same time as a sort of preventive measure.

Keeping plants healthy is a major reason for pruning, hence this kind of remedial work can take place any time of the year. Removing such problems promptly may also prevent their spread to other parts of the garden. 'If you see it, deal with it' is a golden rule.

In a similar vein, removing dead or diseased branches from larger shrubs, and trees especially, is important for the wellbeing of yourself and your possessions as well as for others. A falling branch can do a great deal of harm to passers-by or cars parked underneath, and though this kind of accidental damage is normally covered by most insurance policies, they may argue negligence if you have failed to deal with an obvious problem.

Pruning can also increase the lifespan of a plant, as often old, less vigorous wood is cut out to encourage fresh, new growth.

Pruning keeps plants in check. Left to grow naturally some plants will do their best to take up as much space as they can, often at the expense of anything that happens to be around it. One of the most practical uses of pruning is to keep pathways and access routes clear, as well as windows, doors and roofs in some cases, while less vigorous or diminutive plants may easily be overwhelmed without cutting back stronger plants. This is especially important in smaller gardens where space is at a premium but gardeners want to have a good variety of plants on show. Some plants become a mass of unsightly, tangled growth or become very bare at the base without intervention, while others may just need a lighter trim to ensure they fit well into the display. In a limited scheme every plant has to take up just the right amount of space.

Regular and sensible pruning will also help maintain a plant so that it simply looks better. A good, balanced structure or a uniform shape is rare in nature, but formative pruning and regular attention can achieve such a miracle. No matter whether you prefer the crisp, tight shapes of topiary or the blowsy romance of a climbing rose, your eyes and brain inherently respond to shape, pattern and arrangement. Aesthetics can even be taken one step further, where pruning techniques are used to create art such as David Nash's *Ash Dome*, a sculpture in Wales made from living trees.

More practically, perhaps, pruning is often needed to maximise the best assets of your plants. Many trees and shrubs are grown for a specific reason, whether for foliage shape and colour, flowers or fruit, so it is handy, if not vital, to ensure that these features are amplified. Specific pruning techniques exist to improve a plant's performance, and knowing these will help you get the best out of your garden. Take fruit on a tree, for example, which needs sun to ripen and good air circulation to prevent diseases. Pruning opens up shrubs and trees, allowing sun and air to reach more parts.

## Rambling roses

Despite the naturalistic appearance of a glorious old-fashioned rambling rose clambering over an old tree or a cottage wall, pruning is still required to encourage such an untamed effect. Long, leggy growths that would spoil the appearance need to be cut back whenever they are seen, while once a year a light trim of the whole plant will be required. Every few years a harder prune can take place.

## Bonsai

The Japanese art of bonsai is possibly the most extreme form of controlling a plant, and here it is easy to see how regular pruning over many years can influence growth and shape. Years of careful formative and continuing pruning are required to achieve the final effect. Bonsai may not be suitable for a garden as such, but the techniques used can be applied in a less intense way to garden shrubs and trees.

## Foxglove tree *(Paulownia tomentosa)*

The foxglove tree, if left to grow naturally, can reach heights of around 12m (40ft), producing handsome, lilac, foxglove-type flowers in May. However, many people prefer to pollard it, cutting it back hard annually to encourage fresh shoots and giant, heart-shaped leaves, which can reach almost 60cm (2ft) across. These are quite a sight to behold, even if the flowering display has been sacrificed in the process.

*The foxglove tree, with its huge, luxuriant leaves, is a dramatic addition to any garden.*

### Fruit trees

Fruit tree pruning advice could fill a book by itself. Centuries of growing the beloved apple, for example, have created numerous systems and ways of ensuring the best fruit crop possible. Espaliers are one of the most familiar shapes in country house estates, but work equally well in more modest gardens as they take up very little space, being trained flat against a wall yet still producing abundant fruit. They look fantastic all year round but, with a bit of patience, are surprisingly easy to create.

### *Leylandii* hedges

The fast-growing evergreen Leyland cypress (*Cupressus × leylandii*) is still a popular choice for screening and hedging, but if not kept in check with regular pruning can easily cause enormous problems for anyone living near it.

### Black bamboo

The stems of *Phyllostachys nigra* are a glorious shiny black, but often leaf clusters running up the stem or new weak growth can hide their stunning beauty. Pruning away these excess leaf stalks and thinning out weaker stems will leave a clean, good-looking clump that emphasises the uniqueness of this plant.

### Daphnes

Not all shrubs and trees require automatic attention. Daphnes, as a rule, do not appreciate nor particularly need regular pruning and often suffer dieback if you take a pair of secateurs or shears to them. In some cases knowing when not to prune is as important as knowing when to prune. Dead and diseased stems should still be removed, and in rare cases taking out the odd unruly branch is fine but, on the whole, leave well alone.

# TOOLS FOR PRUNING

Successful pruning relies on having good-quality tools and choosing the right one for the job. Pruning tools need to be safe to use, as the risk of personal injury is high, especially if they are badly maintained or of low quality. Poor tools will also potentially cause damage to your plants, tearing and crushing rather than cutting cleanly, and possibly causing even greater problems than you are trying to rectify by pruning in the first place. Selecting the correct tool is crucial. If a branch does not fit easily into the gap between the blades of your secateurs, switch to something bigger.

## Secateurs

Good secateurs really are a gardener's best friend. Most professional gardeners will carry a good-quality pair of secateurs at all times, hanging off their belt and ready to be used whenever they see a broken branch or a dead flower head.

There are two types of secateurs, anvil and bypass. Anvil secateurs have a sharp blade on one side and a softer, flatter block on the other. The sharp blade cuts through a branch and comes to rest against the block. If not kept impeccably sharp these

*Anvil secateurs (left) have only one sharp blade, while bypass secateurs (right) look more like scissors.*

secateurs may crush the stem rather than cut it, but they require less hand strength to use. Bypass secateurs are more like a pair of scissors on steroids. They should produce a sharper, cleaner cut and in general are easier to use.

Whichever style you choose, look for brightly coloured handles, as this makes them easier to spot, especially when you put them down, and make sure the handles feel comfortable in your hand. Left-handed secateurs and twisting grips can be found, which reduce the strain on the hands and are often used by professional gardeners who are cutting for long periods of time. Check the safety catch and resistance to being squeezed to make sure they suit your hand strength.

## Loppers

For slightly bigger branches, long-handled pruners, usually called loppers, can be used. With their longer handles they are also useful for reaching deeper into a shrub when arms cannot manage it.

The longer the handle the more leverage and force you can exert, which will minimise the effort of cutting, and generally speaking bypass loppers are easier to manipulate over distance than their anvil counterparts.

However, blunt loppers or applying too much force can easily crush stems and branches, leaving behind damage and ragged tears. Trying to cut green and young stems with loppers can also cause crushing rather than cutting. Where loppers are really useful, though, is for quickly removing larger amounts of wood from a shrub, the final clean cuts being undertaken using more manageable tools such as secateurs or a good-quality pruning saw (see opposite).

## Pruning saws

For serious pruning of mature shrubs and trees, nothing beats a good pruning saw. Their size and manoeuvrability mean they can handle awkward and difficult angles much better than long-handled tools can. Pruning saws have either straight or curved serrated blades attached to a handle, and individual blades are usually replaceable. Some blades fold into the handle for safe transport, while others are rigid and fixed. Straight pruning saws are best for cutting through green and sappy wood. Curved blades allow you to apply extra pressure for tougher branches. Whichever saw you choose, safety is important, so look for saws with a scabbard for storage and a good safety catch if you pick the folding type.

## Long-armed saw

It is possible to buy pruning saws with long handles, often extendable, to reach branches above head height without having to climb a ladder. Wearing head and eye protection is also a good idea when cutting above head height, as is checking for overhead wires.

## Long-armed loppers

Again, these are useful for working above head height, although the longer the reach, the more difficult they are to control. The same safeguards should be applied as when using a long-armed saw.

## Bow saw

Bow saws have metal frames shaped like a bow and coarse-toothed blades. Their size makes them difficult to use in congested areas as the energetic to-and-fro motion required can catch and damage other nearby branches. On the whole they are best restricted to cutting branches that are accessible with nothing around them or to cutting wood on the ground removed by other means.

## Shears

For small trimming jobs shears are easy to use and handy. Sharp blades will make them more efficient and produce a cleaner cut, reducing unsightly leaf damage and the amount of effort required. It is also worth checking the pivot strength regularly. Too slack and the shears will fail to cut cleanly, causing bruising and damage; too tight and they will take much more effort to use. Look for shears that are easy to adjust. Those with wavy blades can handle harder shoots better but are more difficult to sharpen.

## Electric hedge trimmer

Although mostly used for hedges, as the name implies, hedge trimmers can sometimes be used on other shrubs for speed and ease without causing too much of a problem. Electric hedge trimmers are lightweight and useful for smaller hedges but do need to be used safely. Keep the electric cable behind you and well out of the way, and never use it in damp or rainy weather or without an emergency circuit breaker, often known as an RCD.

Reciprocating blades, where both blades move over each other, cause less vibration than a single blade moving against a static one, but there is little difference in the cut. Blade length, too, is something to consider, as the longer the blade the heavier it will be but the more quickly you will be able to cut. Usually a 40cm (16in) blade is more than adequate for an ordinary small-to-medium garden.

## Petrol hedge trimmer

These can be much heavier than their electric counterparts but are sometimes necessary for dealing with larger gardens and hedges where electric cables cannot reach, although they are much more tiring to use over long periods. They will also cut through thicker wood more easily without the dreaded 'kicking back' that less powerful electric hedge trimmers are prone to.

## Chainsaws

Chainsaws can be very dangerous tools to use without the proper training. Unless you are willing to put yourself through a professional training course, which can be expensive and time-consuming, it is far better to call in a qualified specialist if the task requires a chainsaw.

## Ladders

For safety reasons it is always better to avoid using a ladder as using cutting tools at height can be a dangerous game. If you do wish to use a ladder, buy a tripod or a platform ladder, which will be much more stable than most stepladders. Always extend it properly, ensure it is level and be careful not to lean out or stretch too far when on it.

### Protective equipment

Thick, sturdy gloves are essential to prevent injuries from sharp tools as well as protecting hands from the scratches and cuts that result from working around spiky, thorny plants or sap, which can irritate skin. Thick gloves, too, should be worn when using vibrating machinery as exposure to vibration can result in nerve damage.

Ear defenders, eye protectors and protective headgear should be worn when using machinery or working above head height.

# TOOL
# MAINTENANCE

## Secateurs and loppers

Plant sap is sticky but soon dries into a hard coating on your blades. Remove by scrubbing with wire wool before rubbing with an oily rag. Oiling the blades and mechanisms of secateurs and loppers will keep them working properly and prevent rust. Secateur blades can be kept sharp using a fine sharpening stone lubricated with a little oil. Push the blade along the stone in one direction only, rather than filing up and down, and remember that the cutting blades should only be sharpened on one side.

## Pruning saws

Use a brush to remove any sawdust trapped in the teeth, which, if left, will reduce the cutting power, then gently rub with wire wool and some lubricating oil before storing. Blades should be replaced once they are no longer cutting cleanly and are becoming an effort to use.

## Hedge trimmers

Always clean the blades with a brush to remove leaves and debris and lubricate with spray or oil before storing. Check that all bolts are secure and that the power cable or engine is in good working condition before using. Ideally you should have such machines serviced yearly by a professional.

# PRUNING BASICS

Before you even think about jumping in with your secateurs, take a bit of time to stand back and take a good look around your shrub or tree. Think about what you are trying to achieve and how you might go about it.

It helps to know a little bit of background botany and understand the way plants grow. This is really the secret of successful pruning practice.

## How plants grow

Plant growth is controlled primarily by hormones called auxins, which are produced in the growing tips of plants and distributed back through the rest of the plant by sap. The higher the level of auxins in the tip, the less the other parts of the plant are likely to grow. So removing the tip of a branch or stem has the effect of temporarily reducing auxin levels, which then usually causes growth to speed up in sideshoots or buds or roots lower down. So pinching out the tip of a young chrysanthemum plant, for example, will result in a much bushier, flower-covered display.

When one branch is dominant over all others, something one can see most easily in young trees, especially conifers, it is known as the leader. Often the leader is very obvious. A Christmas tree is a good example of a plant with high levels of auxin in its leader, resulting in what is known as 'apical dominance'. Remove this tip and you will free the other parts of the plant from their auxin-controlled slavery, though on a Christmas tree, admittedly, this would be unwise. Although auxins have been known about since the 1930s, it has only recently been discovered that this apical dominance of the leader comes about simply because it was the first to grow.

Even if the terminology is tricky, in practical terms this process simply means that if you want a bushier or an open, goblet shape, pruning back the leader should result in exactly the right outcome. On a smaller scale, trimming the tips of bushier plants will have a similar effect, something that we make the most of when growing hedges and screens.

Other plants and shrubs may not have growth lower down to take over if the growing tip is removed. Bare stems without any buds may not respond by putting out shoots, but in most cases new growth should then appear a short time later from ground level.

Looking carefully at the basic overall shape and the way a plant grows can also help you understand what kind of pruning technique will be needed. Most woody plants fall into three categories. The first, the mound-shaped shrubs, have soft, flexible stems and tend to have small leaves. *Spiraea* is a perfect example. The second category of shrubs grow in clumps with individual erect stems rising from the ground, such as forsythia. The third category are tree-like shrubs and trees themselves, of course, which are woodier and have finely divided branches. Witch hazel is a classic example of a tree-like shrub.

Recognising the presence or otherwise of buds is also helpful in gaining pruning confidence. A bud is an undeveloped shoot that usually exists in the axil of a leaf or at the stem tip. Auxins and other hormones control when and how it develops. Buds come in many shapes, sizes and colours and may be obvious, with leaves or flowers growing, or little more than a slight swelling on the stem. The point is these buds are reservoirs of growth just waiting to be activated.

It is worth examining the plants you have in your garden to determine how they grow naturally, before setting about pruning them. Getting familiar with the way plants grow and how buds and shoots look is easier if you do not have the extra worry of whether cutting them off is the right thing to do.

## Basic pruning practices

Some authorities make the distinction between pruning and trimming, although there are not exactly established definitions. At its most basic, if you are removing dead, diseased and damaged or unwanted branches or stems from a plant, you are pruning. If you are cutting back overgrown plants or shaping, you are trimming. Most gardens will need a bit of both during the gardening year

You can also make a similar distinction by separating out 'thinning' activity from 'heading'. Thinning describes removing branches at their point of origin, reducing the density of a plant without stimulating any new growth. 'Heading', removing the top parts of a stem, as already explained, will stimulate growth behind the cut, creating more density and bushiness.

*Pruning is usually a mixture of actions: removing dead wood and crossing or weak branches, as well as trimming and shaping. On this diagram the red marks show where to prune.*

## Cutting back to a bud

It is standard practice in pruning to cut back to a bud wherever possible. This avoids leaving long, unproductive stubs of plant material, which will die back and may invite disease. Sometimes, in certain circumstances, pruning advice might say cut back to a new shoot, to new growth or even to cut back to the ground. Buds on stems tend be either opposite or alternate.

### Opposite buds

Opposite buds literally grow opposite each other on the stem. Hydrangea and *Cornus* are good examples. Prune immediately above a pair of buds, making a flat, clean cut, avoiding knocking off the buds themselves. As these buds grow they will produce two shoots growing in opposite directions from one another.

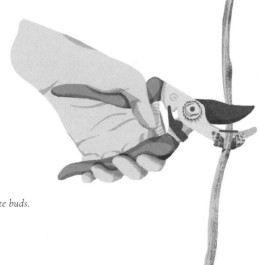

*Pruning opposite buds.*

*Pruning alternate buds.*

## Alternate buds

Other plants, such as roses, have buds that grow alternately along their stems. In this case, try if possible to prune to an outward-facing bud, to minimise future congestion. Make a sloping cut just above the bud, without damaging it, angling it so that any rain will run away from the bud and not towards it. Don't make the slope too steep as this may cause the bud to dry out.

# Other pruning practices

### New shoots
These are in effect buds that have already broken, and it is usually easy to spot their new, fresh growth. Treat them the same way as buds, using a sloping or straight cut as appropriate, but take extra care as they are extremely vulnerable to damage or even to being knocked off. Cutting back to new shoots may be required when pruning winter and early flowering shrubs, as spring growth will have already started.

### New growth
New growth should also be easily recognisable. Young stems are usually thinner, more whip-like and bendy, and generally appear fresher when compared to older growth, which will be woodier-looking and thicker.

### Cutting out
Where growth is completely unwanted, such as a crossing or badly placed branch, it may be better to cut out the entire shoot. This involves tracing it back and cutting it flush at the point where it joins the main stem. This is also sometimes referred to as thinning.

### Cutting to the ground
Some plants benefit from having older stems removed completely to encourage new shoots to grow. The whole stem or branch should be removed as close to ground level as possible rather than to any kind of bud. Usually these older shoots are too thick to be cut with a pair of secateurs, so it is best to use a pruning saw, as it is hard to make clean and level cuts with loppers.

## How much to prune?

In most cases the harder you prune something the more vigorously it will respond. Conversely, lighter pruning means less growth. This is very important to remember especially when trying to balance a lopsided plant. It may feel right to cut the more vigorous side harder than the less vigorous side, but you will actually be encouraging the opposite. So, too, hard pruning a shrub or tree that has outgrown its allotted space may give you a few months' breathing space, but you may well find that it responds by growing even bigger. Indiscriminate and non-selective pruning is never a good idea.

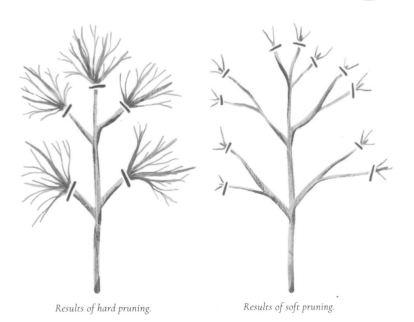

*Results of hard pruning.*     *Results of soft pruning.*

## When to prune?

It may feel that there are as many pieces of advice about when to prune as there are varieties of shrubs and trees. With very few exceptions, you can prune just about any plant or tree at just about any time of the year without doing more than temporary damage. One of the best things about working with perennial shrubs and trees is that they can be very forgiving if one year you get it slightly wrong, and they will no doubt recover sooner or later. In fact there is one school of gardening thought claiming that when it comes to pruning, the right time to prune is when you remember. To a certain extent this is true, and at least proof that pruning is really not the great mysterious ritual that it is sometimes made out to be, but a few simple guidelines will help you to get better results generally and at least make you feel more confident that you are doing the right thing.

Most pruning takes place in late winter or early spring, when rapid growth to replace any removed material is just round the corner. Pruning in summer will suppress the growth of suckers and foliage. It is usually restricted to plants such as apples, grapes and wisteria that have a tendency to produce foliage at the expense of flowers and fruit.

Late summer and autumn pruning can also encourage plenty of regrowth but brings with it the danger of winter damage for new shoots. See pages 64–80 for specific advice on seasonal pruning.

Follow a few basic principles and you should never go too wrong. To begin with, at least make sure you prune at a time when you will not be spoiling the main reason you chose that particular plant in the first place. So, the best time to prune a spring-flowering shrub such as forsythia, for instance, is just after flowering. This gives the shrub almost a whole year to grow back and develop next year's flowering shoots, whereas if you leave pruning to the following winter, those flower buds will have already formed and you will basically just be cutting them off. If in doubt, wait until the flowering and fruiting is finished before undertaking any major pruning activity.

Some pruning, especially shaping and tidying up congestion, is simply easier when plants are dormant. The luxuriant growth of spring and summer leaves can make it hard to see any problem areas or issues, whereas bare branches show off the underlying structure much better. The other major factor with timing is making sure that pruned plants either have enough time to regrow and harden before winter frosts or are pruned when the weather is cold enough to ensure they remain dormant and are not encouraged to start producing new, vulnerable shoots.

## Specific pruning jobs
Over and above the basic principles there are some pruning jobs that can be undertaken at any time of the year, as and when you spot them.

### Cutting out dead, diseased and damaged wood
To avoid spreading infection remove any diseased material as soon as you spot it, no matter the time of year. Cut back a safe distance behind any infection or problem to be on the safe side and clean your tools thoroughly before pruning anything else. A weak solution of bleach or garden disinfectant should do the trick, or whisky, although this would be a terrible waste. Dead wood too can often play host to pests and diseases, which prefer to attack where the plant is weak, plus dead branches can pose a risk to anyone in the vicinity, especially if they are above head height. If you have doubts about whether wood is dead or dormant, scratch a tiny piece of bark off. Living wood will be green and sappy underneath.

Commonly this basic pruning is referred to as the Three Ds – D for dead, D for damaged and D for diseased.

## Crossing branches

When branches grow close together they often begin to rub against each other, especially in windy areas. Over time the bark will rub away, leaving open wounds that can allow the entry of diseases and pests. If left long enough it is quite common for the shrub or tree to callus over the wound, leaving the two branches permanently and naturally grafted together. If disease has not struck then this is not a great problem for the plant itself, but it can look ugly and make it more difficult to prune into a good shape. Ideally, if you spot branches beginning to cross, you should remove what seems to be the weaker of the branches and leave the stronger one. If the two branches are the same size, then use your judgement to decide which one is best to remove.

## Cutting out reversion

Every now and again a beloved variegated shrub will sprout a stem that is not variegated at all. This is known as reversion; when a plant with a specific individual characteristic such as variegated leaves or the twistiness associated with contorted hazel 'reverts' back to a more original standard form. Normally these shoots are stronger than their fancy counterparts and, if left, will gradually take over. This is especially true of variegated reversions, as the green shoots contain more chlorophyll and can therefore photosynthesise at a much higher rate. It is best to cut out reverted shoots completely, whenever they appear, to prevent this takeover.

### Removing suckers

A sucker is a growth, normally strong and vigorous, that emerges from a point low down on a plant, usually where it has been grafted. Roses and fruit trees are often grown this way, with a tough rootstock and a more ornamental top (also known as a scion) joined together, so it is important that the rootstock is not allowed to grow its own shoots. It may well overwhelm the more delicate scion so should be dealt with as soon as possible. If it cannot be pulled away, cut it with the appropriate tool right back to its starting point.

### Pruning twin leaders

Young trees especially may sometimes produce not one but two or more vigorous leaders. Over time they will try and grow away from each other until eventually something will break, especially damaging if the tree has matured. To prevent this, prune out all but the strongest leader at an early stage as soon as you notice it.

### Deadheading

Deadheading is a form of pruning that most people have little problem with. To prevent plants setting seed and to encourage them to produce more blooms, pinch out dead heads or cut them off with a pair of secateurs.

# TREE PRUNING BASICS

For large, mature trees it is always safer to bring in professional help. Using saws and chainsaws, especially when climbing trees, is a dangerous business, and professional tree surgeons go through a great deal of training to ensure they can do the job properly, both for their own safety and others'. A tree that has been pruned badly can topple over in bad weather and can not only harm nearby individuals but also electricity lines, cars and buildings.

In the garden it is possible to tackle smaller pruning jobs, especially when trees are younger and still forming. As tree branches tend to be bigger and heavier than most shrub branches, care must be taken that they do not tear away rather than come off cleanly, leaving ripped bark, splits and ragged edges, which look ugly and may increase the chance of disease. Ideally have someone else hold the branch up while you cut it. If this is not possible use the three-step system used by tree surgeons, developed in the 1980s.

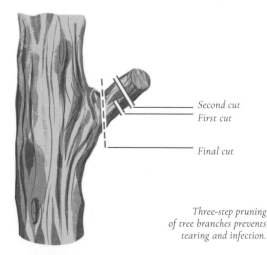

Second cut
First cut

Final cut

*Three-step pruning of tree branches prevents tearing and infection.*

* **First**, cut back the branch in sections if necessary to reduce the overall weight until you have a smallish stump left.
Make an undercut a few centimetres from the trunk, sawing upwards until about the halfway mark. This will help stop the bark tearing.
* Make a **second** complete cut in front of this bottom half cut to remove most of the branch completely.
* Make the **final** cut at a slight angle away from the trunk just in front of the creased ring in the bark (the collar) where the branch meets the trunk.

The branch should come off cleanly, but if some small, jagged splinters remain, clean them up with a pair of secateurs.

Making the cut just in front of the collar means that you are only ever cutting the branch tissue and not the tissue of the remaining stem or trunk, which helps protect the tree from pathogen attack at its heart. It allows the tree to repair itself by producing a protective callus that will eventually cover the wound.

Never be tempted to cut the branch off flush with the trunk for the sake of neatness as this removes the tree's own defence mechanism, without which it cannot heal. This could well lead to unwelcome disease, decay and possibly even death.

Painting the wound, too, a practice common in the past, is also now considered to be dangerous for the tree, preventing the natural process of healing.

# DEALING WITH WASTE

Removing parts of trees and shrubs will inevitably leave you with a disposal issue. Most types of pruning will result in a pile of wood, branches and brushwood as well as greener material, some of which will not easily compost down.

It is more environmentally sound to keep our own waste and recycle it, so although most local authorities have a green waste recycling service this should always be a last resort. There can be charges for green waste collection and disposal, despite the fact that usually the collected waste is processed and sold as a soil conditioner.

The two things you should never do: put green waste into your general waste bin where it will end up in landfill, or dump it anywhere. Throwing garden trimmings over your wall or into the nearest wood, or even worse taking it further afield, is not acceptable. Regardless of how 'natural' your waste is, it still counts as fly-tipping and is illegal, and you may also be doing considerable harm to the environment around you. This is the perfect way to spread disease quickly. You may also be transporting, even if accidentally, seeds and plant material that simply do not belong in the outside environment. If you are tempted, remember that the dreaded Japanese knotweed started off in a garden before it escaped and started its devastating invasion of Britain.

Dumping green waste in the countryside and natural environment may also cause changes to the local ecology, endangering native plants and trees. The nutrients supplied by this unwelcome addition can disrupt the natural balance, which inevitably allows more aggressive plants to thrive at the expense of native plants. This is now a major problem especially in woods and open spaces near to concentrations of human habitation.

# Acceptable methods of disposal

## Composting

Healthy green leaves, small green twigs and shoots can go straight into the compost heap, where they should break down fairly quickly. Bigger branches too, as long as they are cut up into small pieces, will rot down eventually but will need to be mixed with more nitrogen-rich materials such as grass clippings. For larger quantities of green waste or larger branches consider hiring or investing in a chipper. Small, chipped, woody material can then be added to the compost heap, again mixed with greener waste to speed up decomposition. Even so it may take three years or so to rot down fully, but it can then be used as a superb soil conditioner.

## Mulch

If you are not prepared to wait this long, healthy chippings and other pieces can be used as a mulch. Small prunings can be returned back onto borders or under hedges. Chipped waste can be used straight away to mulch paths or borders, although it will temporarily deplete nitrogen around plants, or can be composted separately until well-rotted. This will save having to buy it in.

## Bonfires

Diseased material should always be separated from healthy green waste to ensure that it cannot infect other plants via your home-made compost or mulch. Although bonfires may bring their own environmental issues, burning infected and diseased waste is the only guaranteed way of killing off pathogens. Bonfires do create air pollution, and may well upset your neighbours, so try to minimise their number and effect.

Burn diseased materials when dry to avoid creating thick smoke and always ask your neighbours' permission first, as complaints by others could eventually lead to a fine from the local authority. Be especially careful if you live near a road, as it is an offence to endanger traffic, which is easily done if smoke drifts across a road. A garden waste incinerator is a useful investment, keeping your fire more manageable.

There are also some authorities that suggest burning certain types of wood may be potentially dangerous to health. Cherry laurel, often used for large hedges, contains small amounts of cyanide, so some people worry that burning it could release harmful gases. However, proof of real danger is hard to come by. Try to avoid burning large amounts at once and it makes sense not to breathe in too much smoke, whatever you are burning.

**Logs and branches**
Bigger pieces of wood can be used to create a wildlife refuge. Log piles tucked away in a corner of your garden will offer a welcome home to a variety of beetles, fungi, toads and larger mammals such as hedgehogs. Creating a 'dead hedge' is also an excellent way of dealing with larger amounts of wood and brush. Use a series of upright posts paired up and infill with wood and brush for a wildlife-friendly, rustic-looking barrier.

*A dead hedge is a great way to make use of wood and brush that would otherwise have to be disposed of.*

# LEGISLATION
# AROUND PRUNING

We may think that our homes are our castles, but there are certain rules and regulations around what we do in our gardens that it is worth knowing about. Mostly these laws and guidelines concern either minimising the impact of our gardening activities on the environment or on those around us.

Obviously it should be a rule of thumb, whether there are laws or not, that we do our best to be good neighbours to humans, animals and the environment around us, and that we consider the effects our actions may have and modify those actions wherever they may cause a problem.

## Tree Preservation Orders (TPOs)

A TPO is an order made by a local planning authority in England to protect a specific tree or group of trees that are considered to have a high amenity value, 'amenity' covering a variety of factors. It prohibits the cutting down, hard pruning or damaging of such trees without written permission from the authority, as set out in the Schedule to the Town and Country Planning (Tree Preservation) (England) Regulations 2012. With a few exceptions, if you have a tree in your garden covered by these regulations you do need to seek advice from your local planning office before undertaking any major work or you could face prosecution.

Trees in conservation areas, whether protected or not, are also subject to regulations, and you will usually have to give notice of your intentions if you plan to undertake any major work on your land and wait for consent or otherwise.

## Bonfires

There are no specific regulations against bonfires as such, but certain precautions need to be taken to prevent breaking other laws. Having the odd bonfire may not be a problem but if you choose to have a large one or burn daily you may cause a nuisance to your neighbours, and complaints from them could then be used to prove 'statutory nuisance'. The Clean Air Act 1993 prohibits burning anything that creates dark smoke, and you could be prosecuted if you have knowingly continued with a smoky bonfire. So, too, allowing smoke to drift over a road, or worse, setting fire to the road itself would be an offence under the Highways Act 1980.

## Hedges

Looking after your boundary hedges and trees so that they do not because a problem for others is an important reason to prune regularly and is a polite and neighbourly thing to do. If you ignore your neighbours' rights to enjoy their own property you will possibly end up falling foul of Part 8 of the Anti-social Behaviour Act 2003. This covers the often contentious issue of overgrown or large hedges. Sometimes called the *Leylandii* Law, it requires owners of hedges over 2m (6½ft) tall to take action if they are causing a nuisance to neighbouring properties, although local authority involvement is only a last resort, if all other methods have failed. You do have the right, however, to cut any greenery that is overhanging your property. You must offer the cut material to your neighbour, but they are under no obligation to accept it and you may have to dispose of it yourself. It is an urban myth that you have the right to throw it back over the fence.

Legislation also covers the removal of native hedgerows, permission for which needs to be granted by the local authority. This is most likely to be an issue in rural areas. Pruning and cutting back as such are not prohibited as long as it takes place sensitively.

### Environmental legislation

The Environmental Protection Act 1990 prohibits fly-tipping in any public or open space, and this can include green waste. Other legislation covers destroying wildlife habitats, with bats, badgers, wild birds and many others all having protection. So, for example, removing a decaying tree that is home to a bat colony, or cutting a hedge when you know that birds are nesting within, is an offence under the Wildlife and Conservation Act 1991.

There are also some diseases of woody plants which have to be reported to the authorities. If you think you may have a serious problem in your garden seek professional advice.

# PRUNING
# YOUR PLANTS

# SHRUB PRUNING

Given the wide variety of shrubs available these days this is probably the area that most concerns many gardeners looking for tips on pruning. Fortunately, most shrubs can be grouped together so it is not necessary to be able to remember the right way to prune every individual shrub.

There are some shrubs that have more specific requirements, roses being traditionally treated as a completely separate issue, but these can be learned as and when required. If you don't have roses in your garden you don't need to know all the ins and outs of rose pruning. You can always learn these techniques when you actually need to put them into practice, or simply follow the basic principles of shrub pruning, which will do no real harm.

Regardless of shrub variety, basic pruning actions, such as sucker removal, dealing with dead and diseased material or reversion (see pages 28–29) apply whatever time of the year, as they do to almost every plant. If not done separately these tasks can be undertaken alongside the more species-specific pruning activity.

When tackling any shrub you should begin by having a clear idea of what you are planning to achieve.

Remember that some shrubs are so naturally tidy and ordered in their growth habits, they can almost be left alone. If a shrub is fine and healthy and does not actually need any intervention then you do not need to bother.

## Formative pruning
It is good practice to start your shrubs off well as soon as possible after planting by pruning to ensure a good shape as they mature. In most cases you are probably looking for a good open framework with well-spaced branches and a natural-looking

habit. Evergreen shrubs usually need very little formative training as they tend to have a well-balanced growth habit, so normally it is deciduous shrubs that need the most attention.

Vigorous shoots should be cut back lightly, remembering the rule that hard pruning equals more growth not less. If the entire structure is problematic, cut it back much harder to encourage fresh new growth that you can mould to your liking later on. Otherwise, simply remove any weak, spindly branches or branches that cross.

If a newly planted shrub immediately starts to grow vigorously before the roots have had a chance to spread and anchor the plant, you may want to stabilise it by removing a few stems completely and pruning others back by a third. This will give the roots a better chance of catching up.

*Formative pruning a newly planted shrub.*

# Regular pruning

Many shrubs will never need much more than a check-over for problems, especially if, once established, they do not produce unsightly, vigorous growth or suckering growth from the ground. A little bit of remedial pruning and deadheading can be undertaken to keep them healthy and in good shape.

If you do not want to encourage too much growth but need to reduce the height a little, there are some simple actions you can take. Mounded shrubs can be reduced in size by choosing just a few of the longest branches and cutting them back below the main mass of the shrub, where they will be hidden. For a plant that grows as a clump from the ground, simply remove the longest, tallest stems back to ground level.

The more difficult, tree-like shrubs need a slightly subtler approach. Some branches and growth can be removed completely, while others can be pruned lightly back to a bud. As long as no more than a quarter of the wood is removed the shrub should not react too madly. If you cut back everything indiscriminately you may well end up with a mass of new shoots shooting out from every cut in all directions.

A more routine, seasonal-based pruning may be needed in other cases to maintain or intensify a shrub's ornamental value. Whether grown for its flowers, leaves, stems or fruit, over time the performance of an ornamental shrub often weakens to some degree or other. Of all the types of pruning this is the one that is most seasonally sensitive, requiring at least a little knowledge about growth patterns.

Shrubs that flower at different times of the year are pruned in order to maximise their seasonal flower display and fruit if this is important. The crucial factor involved in pruning flowering shrubs at the right time is the kind of growth they flower on.

*Most shrubs need only a light prune to look good.*

Those shrubs that flower on new growth, such as *Buddleja* and *Tamarix*, should be pruned in late winter or early spring to encourage plenty of fresh, new flowering shoots for a good summer display. If left they will gradually grow leggier over time, with fewer flowers. The same applies to shrubs grown for attractive leaves, which are inevitably more exciting when young and fresh.

Shrubs that flower on older, more mature wood, forming a permanent framework, are generally hard pruned after flowering to ensure the maximum amount of growing time before the next season's flowers, or more lightly pruned when dormant, which allows you to better pinpoint exactly where the flowers are produced; at the tips, sideshoots or off the main stem. In order to keep these shrubs tidy you can cut back most of the previous year's flowering growth to within a few buds of old wood. Once they are established you can also remove a few of the oldest stems annually to ease congestion and encourage fresh stems to

*Pruning suckering and clump-forming plants prevents congestion.*

grow. This should prevent them from becoming top-heavy. At the same time remove weak branches and thin out congested stems, especially those that are crossing.

Suckering shrubs and clump-formers such as *Kerria* are treated a little differently as, although they flower on old wood, they make lots of new growth from the ground each year and can easily become very congested. Once established, all flowering shoots should be cut back hard after they have flowered, staggering the lengths slightly, while a quarter to a third of the older shoots can be cut back to just above ground level.

## Evergreen shrubs

Evergreen shrubs are most likely to need pruning after being damaged by frost. Hard winters can cause dieback, often on one or other side, which is unsightly and a possible entry point for disease. If this is the case, prune out all dead wood back to wherever there are signs of regeneration, so it is preferable to do this around mid-spring when any new growth should be obvious. Hopefully your shrub will recover in time.

Most medium to large evergreen shrubs should rarely need pruning if they have received good early formative pruning and have a good balanced framework. Dead or diseased and damaged branches, crossing branches and any longer, straggly growth can be removed to keep them healthy and well-shaped, or they can be trimmed for a more formal effect.

## Renovating shrubs

You may find yourself having to tackle plants that have to be dramatically reduced in size. Even if you have assiduously kept your own patch under control you might one day move house or inherit someone else's garden. Perhaps you have to cut something back for less life-changing reasons, such as having a wall repainted or repaired or, most likely, the shrubs you planted in good faith simply turned out to be a little bigger than you imagined or just did their own thing while you were not looking.

There are a few considerations to think about when making such a big decision.

* Not all plants will recover from really hard pruning.
* Be careful with your timing. This kind of really hard pruning is best done in early spring, just before bud break, to make the most of the natural spring growth spurt.
* Be prepared for the final appearance and result. Hard pruning will take some time to recover so a boundary hedge will not do its job of providing privacy and security for some time.
* You will need to take extra care afterwards, with extra food and water to ensure healthy regrowth.

## Complete renovation

There is something rather satisfying in tackling an overgrown border, removing all that thick, gloomy density to leave just a few trunks and branch stubs, and in the vast majority of cases trees and shrubs can take this kind of hard pruning without dying off. The few that do not, such as hebes, daphnes and some rhododendrons, can always be replaced if time and resources mean that this wholesale destruction is necessary.

This kind of renovation is popular with landscapers and builders and requires no special skill, as almost all growth is removed, leaving only 15– 25cm (6–10in) of trunk or stem above ground.

## Gradual renovation

Renovation over several years is less catastrophic than a complete cutback and may be better for shrubs that are less inclined to recover quickly or for those that are very visible.

  * In year one a third of the oldest and most unproductive branches are removed.
  * In year two half of the remaining old branches are removed.
  * In year three all remaining old branches are removed. The remaining branches should now be young, healthy growth.

*Complete renovation.*          *Gradual renovation.*

# TREE PRUNING

Pruning mature landscape trees is a job best left to the professionals, but keeping more ornamental garden trees in check should be within the bounds of a gardener's capability. Tree pruning has its own language, but that should not put you off learning how to make the best of the trees you have. They may well be the most expensive purchase you have made for your garden and certainly will be the most long-lasting if treated well. Not only that, but trees are often important focal points in a garden. Most of us do not have the space and land to grow a grove of trees, let alone a wood, so presumably the one or two trees that we have space for really need to look good and justify their place.

In any case, it makes ecological sense to avoid major work on old, mature trees unless there are real safety issues. They play host to wildlife of all types that has evolved over time to coexist with trees in all their various stages of growth and decay, and ideally should be left as untouched as possible.

*A tree with a central leader shape.*

*A goblet-shaped tree.*

## Formative pruning

Starting a young tree off properly is the single most important pruning activity you can undertake. The idea is to create a good, well-balanced structure of evenly spaced branches plus a strong trunk.

Most very young trees are sold as feathered trees, with a single, central leader and lots of sideshoots along the main stem. After planting, cut out any badly placed sideshoots and any that are weak or damaged, leaving a well-spaced basic tree shape. If evergreen, this is probably the only pruning you will have to do. If there are signs of another leader developing, remove this too. Competing leaders can cause real problems later on as the joint between the two is often weak and can split open. Otherwise prune similarly over the next few years to keep a good shape.

Central-leader standards are very similar except that more of the lower branches are removed to leave a clear, visible trunk, and your yearly pruning should continue this. Encouraging a good length of trunk is useful if your tree's main attraction is coloured or interesting bark, in which case it is advisable to remove any low-placed branches and smaller side branches over a number of years, leaving you with a more distinctive, elegant branch shape to show off the ornamental bark.

For a more open-centred, goblet-shaped tree the central leader may have already been removed, or you can do this yourself as soon as the tree has grown a good, strong, even framework of sideshoots. Without the dominance of the leader these will grow more strongly and, if pruned to an outward bud thereafter, continue to frame an open goblet shape. Any strong vertical growth should also be cut out to ensure it does not become a new leader.

Trees bought in containers from the garden centre will probably have already had some formative pruning at the nursery. You can, however, prune after planting if there are any issues.

# Regular pruning

Once an ornamental tree is well established there is usually little need for extra pruning. Congested, crossing and dead branches can be removed if you can reach them safely, along with inward-growing branches or any branches that spoil the shape, as long as this does not ruin the overall balance. If in doubt use a professional tree surgeon.

Hard pruning an established tree that has outgrown its space will probably do more harm than good, leading to a congested mass of water shoots, the thin, upright twiggy growths that suck energy away from flowering and fruiting, or a host of suckers lower down the trunk. Rather than prune a tree hard all in one go, prune it more gently over two or three years, gradually removing old growth and controlling the new replacement growth to keep a good shape. Some species of tree are worse than others for producing a mass of shoots after pruning, so it might be better to leave well alone in some cases.

# Raising the canopy

Where a tree casts too much shade or has lower branches hanging down where they can be a nuisance, you can lift the canopy by pruning off the lower branches. It is not wise to lift too high as this could easily make the tree top-heavy and vulnerable to toppling in bad weather. The golden rule is that the trunk should be no more than a third of the tree's overall height. This is also more aesthetically pleasing. Even conifers, which often have side branches from top to bottom, can be raised in this way.

## Pruning fruit trees

Trees that are grown for their fruit, such as apple trees, for example, have their own special pruning regime, dealt with on pages 59 and 67.

49

# PRUNING CLIMBERS

Climbers offer a gardener a whole different plane to work with and can be one of the most creative elements in garden design, bringing vertical style as well as covering the ugly or unwanted. Often, though, they can be naturally unruly. Born to clamber over everything in their path, they may simply stretch too far towards the light. In most gardens their growth needs to be controlled and restrained for the sake of other nearby plants or features and to ensure that they continue to flower year after year. So regular pruning is pretty much essential for nearly all established climbers.

Pruning and training go hand in hand when it comes to managing most climbers as many, despite their name, need support to grow upwards properly.

## Formative pruning

As soon as possible after planting a climber you should begin the pruning and training process. Pick the strongest-looking shoots to tie in to their support. If they have few or no sideshoots, trim them back to a strong bud to encourage better growth lower down. Continue to tie them in as they grow, and prune out any shoots that are growing in the wrong direction if they have become too woody to be trained vertically. Trimming back the growing tip of a shoot higher or lower down the stem as required will help you balance out your climber.

## Regular pruning

Once established nearly all climbers require some form of pruning to keep them in check or prevent them from continually growing upwards. There are certainly a few well-loved garden climbers that have quite specific pruning requirements, such as wisteria and clematis.

Generally, when to prune an established flowering climber follows similar rules to shrub pruning in that it is dictated by flowering time and growth method. Those climbers that flower on the current season's growth in summer are pruned when dormant in late winter or early spring to promote plenty of fresh shoots. Those that flower on older, more mature growth are pruned immediately after flowering to give the maximum amount of time for any new shoots to mature. At the same time it is wise to remove any weak, damaged stems and any congestion and twiggy growth. You can also remove any shoots that have outgrown their space to limit the height and spread of your climber.

The same principle applies to any flowering evergreen climber. Prune only after flowering to ensure a good display the following season. Non-flowering evergreens can be pruned in summer, so that any new shoots that result have a chance to harden before winter sets in.

Old and neglected climbers are often little more than a mass of bare, tangled woody stems but can usually be renovated by cutting back hard almost to the ground or, if they are not so vigorous, by hard pruning sections over several years.

# PRUNING SMALL SHRUBS AND SUB-SHRUBS

It's all too easy to think of pruning as something that controls the growth of big shrubs in the garden. Yet there are a whole host of ground-hugging and smaller dwarf shrubs, often called sub-shrubs, which also need attention to give of their best.

Usually this is where a pair of shears really comes into its own. The smaller-sized twiggy growth, the mass of small flower heads and the lack of thick wood mean that pruning saws and even secateurs are just not necessary. Unlike bigger shrubs, these types of plants have no strong framework to thin, and by their very nature are often dense and congested. But this is how they grow.

There are a number of small shrubs in this category that need nothing more than a light trim as they do not tend to regrow if you cut back into the older, woody growth. Ideally, if you prune them regularly, once a year at least, you can prevent the plant growing too much old wood. It will look fresher and more attractive this way and flower better for you.

Ground cover shrubs such as *Hypericum calycinum* and *Helianthemum*, for example, can be sheared over hard each spring, removing almost all the previous season's growth to keep them from becoming straggly.

Varieties of *Vinca*, too, can be cut back annually if necessary, especially if you need to keep them in check. Shear off all the older stems, leaving any short, upright new growth to develop. This is one job that is sometimes easier with secateurs depending on how much growth you have to deal with.

Heathers are often used as ground cover, for their dense, weed-suppressing foliage and their natural tidiness and sensible habit, as much as for their bright flowers. Ericas, which flower in winter and early spring, can be lightly trimmed with shears after flowering, cutting just below the spent flower heads. Do not cut back hard into old wood as this is one of those plants that will not regenerate from old wood. *Calluna*, the Scottish heather, flowers in late summer. It too can be trimmed in early spring ready for the new season, shearing off the flower heads and the tips of the shoots without cutting back into old wood.

As with their larger cousins, cut out any dead or diseased shoots whenever you come across them. It is usually preferable to cut them right back to the ground and let the foliage around grow to hide the inevitable gap.

# HEDGES

Hedges and screens are an important feature of many gardens, providing protection from weather and intruders as well as helping to divide and frame garden sections. They are especially useful in exposed areas as windbreaks, filtering wind and reducing its speed, and for protecting more delicate plants from the cold.

All hedges need some attention, but quite how much and how often does depend on the type of hedging plant used. Informal hedges usually require less attention than more formal ones, which are often, though not exclusively, evergreen, and by their very nature have to look clean and clipped throughout the year. It is always worth remembering too that the faster-growing a hedge is – however useful this might be in the early days – the more it will need to be trimmed regularly as it matures.

## Formative pruning

After planting deciduous hedges, cut them back by a third to encourage plenty of bushy new growth outwards as well as upwards, and repeat this over several years so that the hedge is as dense at the bottom as at the top. Evergreen hedges are usually only trimmed at the sides, leaving the top to grow up to the desired height before being squared off. This too will help create a good, dense base. Continue this for several years, as necessary, rather than trying to increase the height of the hedge too quickly.

Even at this early stage try to develop a base that is slightly wider than the top as this helps to deflect wind and protect hedges from heavy snowfall. This angled shape is known as 'the batter' and is standard practice, especially for dense, formal hedges.

*Hedges and screens are an important*
*component of many gardens.*

# Regular pruning

## Formal hedges

Once formal hedges have reached the required height they can be trimmed all over to maintain a good shape. Some, such as beech and hornbeam, need trimming once a year, towards the end of summer, while yew and box hedging ideally need trimming several times during the growing season. The faster-growing hedges, including *Leylandii*, need more trimming still.

You can prune formal hedges to have a flat top, a rounded top or even a tapering, A-shaped top.

The best way to trim a flat top and make sure it is perfectly level is to set up a line first. Tie a length of string between two posts and pull taut at the height you want. Keep your shears or hedge trimmer at the same level as this guideline as you move along the hedge. Shears need to be kept as horizontal as possible

*A hedge is more stable if the base is wider than the top.*

to ensure a level cut. This is usually a little easier to manage with a hedge trimmer, which should be used in a wide, sweeping arc away from the body.

Flat tops are often used on yew or privet and suit plants with a very dense growth habit. Lower-growing box hedges are also shaped this way, although not necessarily with angled sides due to their size. You can also use a string line to trim the sides of your hedge more accurately.

Rounded tops are recommended for less dense conifers. They too protect the hedge from bad weather but have a gentler appearance. For a really accurate shape you can use a wooden template, although most people can manage a reasonable curve by eye. This also applies to an A-shaped top, which is useful in areas with heavy snowfall.

### Informal hedges

Even though informal hedges have a more relaxed, natural shape, they will need some attention to keep them under control. Flowering hedges, such as rose and forsythia, can be lightly cut back after flowering.

### Renovating hedges

With the exception of yew, conifers do not respond to hard pruning. Most other hedging plants, however, will handle hard pruning if they have grown out of shape or are too large. Hedge renovation should ideally be undertaken over two years. Cut back growth to the main stem on one side only and cut the top down to the preferred size in the first year, but wait to cut the other side until the second year.

## Renovating a beech hedge *(Fagus sylvatica)*

* Decide what size you want your overgrown hedge to be after renovation and set up a string attached to two posts as a guideline to work to.

* Remove dead and diseased branches first, then cut back thick branches using loppers or a pruning saw to just below the width or height you want. Use secateurs to trim back any smaller branches that remain.

* Cut along the top and down one side only in the first year.

* Feed and mulch in spring to encourage good growth.

* Leave pruning the other side until the following year to avoid placing too much stress on your plants.

* Also useful for: hornbeam, yew, privet, *Lonicera nitida*.

*Renovating a beech hedge.*

# FRUIT PRUNING

## Fruit trees (top fruit)

Apples and pears are treated in exactly the same way when it comes to pruning. Free-standing trees are traditionally pruned in winter, mainly because it is easier to see the shape and structure of the tree, but also because commercial fruit growers generally have more time on their hands at this time of year. However, gardeners and fruit growers are recognising that more vigorous trees can benefit from being pruned once they have come into growth (spring and summer) to try to dissipate some of their energy. There is a saying that an apple tree has been pruned enough once a pigeon can fly through the centre of the canopy without its wings hitting any of the branches. The theory is that when pruning, it is important to leave plenty of space between the branches, to allow air to circulate and to allow maximum sunlight to reach the flower buds and emerging fruit.

Members of the *Prunus* family are the other most popular fruit trees grown in the garden. They include cherries, damsons, apricots, peaches and almonds. These trees should never be pruned in winter as the wounds leave them susceptible to diseases such as silver leaf and bacterial canker. Instead they should be pruned any time between mid-spring and early autumn. Plums and damsons do not require much pruning, just occasionally removing a branch to prevent overcrowding within the canopy, or to reduce the weight of a branch, as they are prone to snapping when overladen with fruit.

Cherries are divided into two categories, sweet and sour. Sweet varieties produce fruit on short, fruiting spurs, so sideshoots should be pruned back to a few buds to encourage more spurs to emerge. Sour cherries fruit on branches produced the previous year, so some of the older wood should be pruned back and replaced with younger branches. Peaches are treated exactly the same as sour cherries.

## Soft fruit

Gooseberries, redcurrants and whitecurrants have very similar growth habits to each other and are pruned in the same way. They are usually grown as an open-centred bush on a short leg or stem. They fruit both on old branches and at the base of the new growth. The main pruning season is in winter. Thin out stems growing from the centre of the canopy to leave about five or six branches spaced out equally from the centre. Tip the leaders of these branches back by about a third. Prune back new growth on any sideshoots to about two buds.

Blackcurrants fruit differently to their cousins, the redcurrants, by cropping on young new growth as opposed to older wood. They are grown as stool bushes, meaning they are planted just below the soil surface, and encouraged to produce vigorous young shoots, which emerge from below the soil. Pruning takes place in winter, using loppers or secateurs to remove about a fifth of the older shoots at ground level, leaving predominantly younger, vigorous shoots to crop that season.

Raspberries are divided into two categories. Summer-fruiting raspberries fruit on stems produced the previous year. Cut back canes after they have fruited down to ground level and tie in new ones that will fruit the following year. Autumn raspberries fruit on canes produced in the same year. Cut all growth back down to ground level in early spring to encourage vigorous, fruiting canes for cropping in late summer and autumn.

Blackberries and hybrid berries should be trained in the same way as summer raspberries, leaving stems produced the previous year to bear the crop.

Blueberries are pruned in a similar fashion to blackcurrants, by pruning some of the older wood back to ground level each winter using loppers, and encouraging new shoots to grow from the base.

*A typical open-centred soft fruit bush.*

# PRUNING
# THROUGH
# THE SEASONS

# WINTER PRUNING

Winter is a good time to prune many deciduous shrubs and trees as it is easier to see the bare structure and identify problems. Hard pruning and renovating overgrown shrubs and hedges can also be a winter task, when there is more time to do a thorough job and less competition for your attention as there would be at other times of the year.

## Tree pruning

A wide range of trees can be pruned in winter, including those with ornamental bark and apple and pear trees. Avoid pruning fruiting trees from the *Prunus* family, such as cherries and plums, or rowans, as they are especially prone to bacterial and fungal infections at this time.

### Pruning an *Acer davidii*

* Remove any sideshoots that are growing off the trunk up to the height you want.
* Remove any dead, diseased or damaged shoots or branches.
* Remove any crossing, thin branches to leave a clear, balanced shape.
* Other small trees to prune this way: *Acer griseum, Betula utilis var. jacquemontii, Cornus kousa.*

*Opposite:
Strikingly beautiful
bark on an
Acer davidii.*

*Pruning an* Acer davidii.

# Shrub pruning

Winter is an excellent time to hard prune any shrubs, deciduous or evergreen, other than conifers, which have outgrown their space or become misshapen. Towards the end of winter it is also possible to begin to prune flowering shrubs ready for the coming growing season. The danger with beginning this pruning too early is the threat of cold and frost damaging any new growth that results, but if you are confident in the stability of your local weather conditions it helps to spread the workload.

## Renovating an overgrown *Mahonia × media* 'Charity'

Prune as flowering finishes if possible.

* Prune back long stems a little at a time to roughly 60cm (2ft).
* Remove any dead, diseased or crossing growth.
* Cut out old growth, leaving five or six strong and well-balanced stems.
* Cut back these remaining stems to about 30–40cm (12–16in) above the ground. Slope the cuts slightly to allow rain to run off.
* New growth should appear later in the year, but flowering may be delayed for a couple of years.

*Hard pruning works well on many overgrown shrubs.*

\* Keep plants short and bushy by regularly removing spent flower heads in the future.

\* Other shrubs that respond to hard pruning: *Philadelphus, Abelia, Choisya, Forsythia, Viburnum tinus, Aucuba japonica.*

\* Avoid hard pruning *Ceanothus, Daphne, Cytisus* and *Genista.*

## Pruning climbers

Winter is an excellent time to deal with vigorous wall climbers like ivy and Virginia creeper, removing any longer shoots and growth near to windows, doors and gutters. Wisteria too should also be pruned at this time, followed by an extra summer prune. See page 78 for detailed instructions.

## Pruning an open-centred apple tree

Apple tree pruning is really not as complicated as it may at first seem if you just follow a few basic principles, as outlined below. All fruit experts will probably prune their trees slightly differently, with regards to which individual branches they remove. Just remember the overall effect and shape required and what you are trying to achieve: to produce more flowers, which will result in more fruit. On a typical, average tree, aim to remove about a tenth of the branches, although this will vary from tree to tree. The best time for pruning to allow you to see the overall shape of the tree is in winter.

\* Remove any branches growing from within the centre of the tree to reduce congestion and allow more air to circulate. This will minimise pest and disease problems.

\* Work your way around the tree, looking to remove diseased or dead branches.

\* Now look to remove crossing or rubbing branches. Remember, when removing a branch always cut back to another lower branch or trunk. Never leave a stub. Also, remove one of the branches if it looks as though some are in close proximity to each other and are going to cast shade.

\* If there is any, remove some of the upright, vigorous new growth. This is unlikely to bear fruit in the future, but instead will cause shade and prevent other branches from fruiting.

\* Cut back some of the sideshoots to encourage spurs to form. If the tree is a tip-bearing type (look at the tips of the new shoots to see if large fruit buds are there, which will show it is a tip-bearer), remove whole branches, and don't prune too many sideshoots back as this will result in a loss of crop.

\* Cut back the leaders (the shoots at the end of each branch) by about a third to encourage more fruiting sideshoots and spurs to form.

*Removing sideshoots (left), branch tips (centre) and inward-facing branches (right).*

# SPRING PRUNING

Spring is a busy time of the year in the garden, and there are plenty of activities to keep the gardener occupied, so it makes sense to prioritise jobs and spread them out over the period. Some pruning tasks are more necessary than others. Concentrate on these first.

## Tree pruning

Most trees are best pruned in summer or winter, with the exception of evergreens such as *Magnolia grandiflora* and holly that prefer spring. Concentrate on these and on removing damage caused by winter cold and frost.

## Shrub pruning

Shrubs grown for winter stem interest are normally cut back in early spring to ensure good colour on the new shoots. Some, like *Rubus cockburnianus*, can be almost completely cut back to the ground. Others are coppiced or pollarded, although the effect of renewing fresh, more colourful young growth is the same in all cases.

### Pruning white-stemmed bramble *(Rubus cockburnianus)*

* Cut back all the previous season's shoots to a few centimetres above the ground.
* Wear thick, sturdy gloves, as these plants are very thorny.
* Also try with: *Rubus biflorus*, *Lespedeza*.
* Most roses are also pruned in early spring, and more details about this can be found on page 81.
* Winter and early spring flowering shrubs can be pruned once flowering is over.

**Pruning Chinese witch hazel (Hamamelis)**

* Prune witch hazels just as the flowers are fading, but before leaves arrive.
* Prune back any tall, leggy growth by a third. Look for old rather than new growth to cut out.
* Cut out any dead, diseased or crossing branches and any weak growth.
* Step back and check the overall shape, which should be evenly balanced and open-centred.
* Reduce or remove stems bit by bit until you are happy with the result.
* Other shrubs that can be pruned in early spring: deciduous viburnums, *Corylopsis*, *Chimonanthus*, winter-flowering jasmine, winter-flowering honeysuckle.

*Witch hazels are pruned in early spring.*

## Pruning *Buddleja davidii*

One of the easiest shrubs to prune is *Buddleja davidii*, or the butterfly bush, which is cut back hard to encourage plenty of flowers and prevent it from growing leggier and leggier year after year.

* Prune back each of the previous year's stems to two or three buds above last season's growth.
* Other species of *Buddleja*, such as *B. globosa*, need only a light pruning.
* Other summer-flowering shrubs that benefit from hard pruning in spring include: hardy fuchsia, *Hypericum*, *Lavatera*, *Perovskia*, *Tamarix* and also *Cotinus* for a good display of leaf colour.

*Buddlejas are cut back hard to encourage plenty of new flowering growth.*

**Shrubs that flower on current season's growth**
Spring, when the sap is rising and growth rates are at their
highest, is the best time to prune shrubs that produce flowers
on the new season's growth. Hard pruning at this time, in
many cases, should ensure a really good flowering display
later on in summer.

**Shrubs that benefit from light trimming in spring**
Other summer-flowering shrubs can be lightly trimmed,
removing any old flower heads, crossing branches and dead or
diseased material. In all cases aim for a clean, uncongested shrub.
  A light trim in spring will benefit *Amelanchier, Gaultheria,*
heather, *Rhamnus, Potentilla* and *Cistus.*

**Climbers**
Certain types of clematis – those that flower in early summer or
late summer to autumn – are best pruned in spring. See page 85
for more details. Honeysuckle and ivy can also be pruned at this
time, being careful not to disturb any nesting birds.

**Hedges**
Wildlife hedges, containing plants like blackthorn, hazel and
hawthorn, should be pruned early in spring before birds start
nesting in order to ensure better flowering and fruiting later on.

# COPPICING AND POLLARDING

Coppicing and pollarding are traditional methods of harvesting wood from trees. Today, however, these techniques are more commonly used in the garden to emphasise the special characteristics of certain plants.

## Coppicing

Some varieties of dogwood and willow are grown primarily for their winter stem colour. Cultivars range from bright green to orange and red. The colour is strongest on new growth and fades as the wood ages, so these plants are cut down annually just before the new leaves form, or every two years, to ensure a better flush of colour.

### Coppicing *Cornus alba* 'Sibirica'

* Cut back each stem to an outward-facing bud about 5cm (2in) above the previous year's cut.
* Once all the stems have been cut back you should be left with a framework no more than 30cm (12in) high.

* Other shrubs that can be coppiced: *Cornus alba* cultivars, *Salix alba* var. *vitellina* 'Britzensis', variegated elder, twisted hazel, common hazel.

*Shrubs grown for winter colour should be coppiced regularly.*

# Pollarding

Pollarding is a traditional method of keeping the growth of large trees such as limes in check but is also found on a smaller scale in the garden. Pollarding is similar to coppicing, the main difference being that old stems are cut back to a central trunk. This requires allowing the shrub or tree to develop a trunk or central stem first before annually pruning old shoots to encourage a head of new growth at the top.

### Pollarding *Paulownia tomentosa*

* Remove any weak growths completely to make it easier to reach any thicker stems.
* Cut back all old strong stems to a couple of buds from the main trunk. Remove any crossing, diseased or dead stems as you work around.
* Once finished *Paulownia* should look a little like a lollipop. The new sprouts will have huge, velvet heart-shaped leaves, although there will be no flowers.
* Other plants to pollard: *Salix, Cotinus, Eucalyptus.*

*Pollarding a* Paulownia tomentosa *(foxglove tree).*

# SUMMER PRUNING

The summer season is all about keeping everything looking good. Trimming formal hedges and topiary and deadheading roses and other flowering shrubs are the main jobs at this time of year, but summer is also an opportunity to prune many trees.

## Trees
Trees that have been left in winter can be pruned as necessary during the summer months. Cherries, plums and rowans are now less prone to infection.

## Shrub pruning
Continue to prune deciduous flowering shrubs when their display is over.

## Evergreen shrubs
Most evergreen shrubs need little pruning except for a tidying up of straggly shoots and removal of dead or diseased material including old flowers. Camellias and Rhododendrons can be tidied up in summer although camellias can also, if necessary, be hard pruned when they have become too big.

## Climbers
Spring-flowering clematis can be pruned in summer if they have become too big or tangled but are otherwise best left alone, except to remove any dead or damaged wood.

Wisteria do appreciate a summer prune, however. Details on page 78.

# Summer hedge cutting

Formal hedges of yew and box will need clipping several times during the summer months to keep their shape. More informal and boundary hedges can be left to late summer or, if full of berries, pruned in spring to help wildlife.

## Trimming a formal yew hedge

* After a light trim in spring, yew will benefit from a proper trim in summer to keep compact and tidy. Yew can grow as much as 30cm (12in) in a year so needs to be cut back to where it was pruned previously or it will gradually expand its waistline.
* Depending on the size of the hedge, shears or a hedge trimmer to trim the sides first.
* Remember to angle the cut so the hedge is wider at the bottom than the top, and cut as straight as you can.
* Cut the top of the hedge using a line of string as a guide. Use a safe ladder or platform if you are working at height.
* To prevent leaning over too much while cutting, cut the nearest half of the top first, then work from the other side.
* Make sure the corners look especially crisp and precise to finish the look, or round them off gently for a less formal appearance.
* Do the same for box, privet, *Lonicera nitida*.

# AUTUMN PRUNING

As a rule it is better not to prune trees and most shrubs in autumn as the higher levels of humidity and the abundance of fungal spores in the air can increase the risk of infection. Deciduous shrubs and trees, too, are preparing for dormancy and will be slower to repair any pruning wounds.

Flower heads of shrubs that have a reputation for self-seeding, such as *Buddleja*, can be pruned in autumn, as this will help prevent future problems. Autumn is, however, an excellent time to prune rambling and climbing roses whilst they still have some sap in their system and are pliable and easier to train up supports. See page 83 for details. Hybrid tea and floribunda roses can be reduced by a third to prevent wind rock over winter.

## Pruning lavender

Beautiful and evocative though it is, pruning lavender can become somewhat of a bugbear for many gardeners. They are shrubs which can easily become leggy and split, often developing a woody, unsightly base topped by a mauve Mohican haircut. Yet it is a golden rule that you cannot cut back into this old wood.

Whether you are growing lavender as a hedge or a stand-alone shrub, the answer is to prune twice a year. The first cut is really little more than deadheading. In late summer use secateurs or shears to remove all the spent flower heads, cutting them back, stalks and all just below the line of the foliage.

In spring, just before the plants wake from their winter dormancy, cut them back harder, as close as possible to the old wood without actually cutting into it. Try and shape your lavenders into something resembling a large football, as this will help the sides grow new foliage and prevent the plants from becoming leggy. Always try to avoid cutting flat along the top as this will increase the amount of wood on show, which can look very unsightly. Pruning in this way will help keep your lavender bushy for longer and will encourage many more flowers.

## Pruning wisteria

Wisteria can be a self-indulgent, vigorous grower, preferring to produce a mass of whippy green growth over the flowers that we love so much. Pruning wisteria is not difficult if you remember this. The overall aim is to control the leafy growth in summer and encourage the plant to put its energy into producing flower buds instead. Winter pruning is more about promoting a good framework of largely horizontal branches as these will produce the most flowers.

In late summer cut back long main and sideshoots leaving 4–6 leaves, being careful not to damage any buds. If you need to extend the framework of your wisteria leave some shoots unpruned and train them in.

In winter cut back the spurs created last summer once again, leaving only two to three buds and reduce any longer shoots that may have developed since the summer prune.

*Summer pruning of wisteria.*          *Winter pruning of wisteria.*

# Pruning hydrangea

Classic shrubs in the garden, hydrangeas come in a variety of shapes and sizes. The mophead hydrangeas are probably the most familiar but other species are increasingly popular for their fantastic flowering display. There is even a climbing hydrangea, an incredibly useful wall climber that can thrive even on a north-facing wall.

Different species of hydrangea have slightly different pruning requirements.

### Hydrangea arborescens

These deciduous shrubs are renowned for their enormous pompom flower heads in white or pink. For maximum-sized flowers they should be hard pruned almost back to the ground in early spring, although cutting a little less harshly will give you a bushier plant with smaller flowers.

### Hydrangea paniculata

These are plants that flower on the current season's growth and are a wonderful addition to the late summer garden. The elegant cones are usually white, but lime-green cultivars are currently in vogue.

* Pruning is required in late winter or early spring simply to keep the plants compact.
* Prune last season's stems to one or two buds from their base as well as removing any dead, diseased, crossing and weak branches.
* Try to ensure that the shrub is well-balanced and open to make the best framework for the flowering stems.

*The correct way to prune* Hydrangea macrophylla.

### Hydrangea macrophylla

One of our most beloved shrubs, *Hydrangea macrophylla*, with its colours ranging from white through pink and blue to purple, and its tolerance for dappled shade, is very useful in the garden.

Their flowers are formed the previous year so the timing and quality of pruning is very important. Cutting them back too hard will just result in the loss of most of the flower buds. Allowing the spent flower heads to remain on the plant through winter will help protect those buds from the worst of the cold weather.

Only prune when the danger of hard frost has passed. Remove the old flower heads, cutting back to the next pair of strong buds. Avoid hard pruning as this will remove future flowers. One or two old stems can be pruned out occasionally to promote new growth.

### Hydrangea petiolaris

The climbing hydrangea requires little pruning. Old flower heads can be removed after flowering and any long, straggly stems cut out in early spring. These hydrangeas can be hard pruned in spring if they have outgrown their space.

# PRUNING ROSES

The mysteries of rose pruning can feel like some sort of arcane ritual that only the initiated can fully understand. Centuries of obsessional breeding, and perhaps centuries of gardeners trying to outdo one another, have made the whole thing sound quite complicated. So it is always worth remembering that roses are relatives of the bramble. If you have ever hacked back a rampant blackberry then you will have no problem handling a rose.

The secret is to know the kind of rose you are dealing with. Once you have a handle on that, the basic pruning techniques are not that different from those of other plants, albeit with more thorns. Alternatively you can always grow roses that need very little care. Species roses, the closest in growth pattern to the bramble, can be treated like any other flowering shrub, while modern English roses have been bred to perform without too much attention and are increasingly popular.

Finally, although traditional techniques are still out there, the last 20 years or so have seen a huge change in thinking, following experiments with different, less complex methods of pruning. It seems that roses will perform perfectly well if you just take a hedge trimmer to them! Nothing arcane about that.

## Traditional methods of rose pruning

### Hybrid teas and floribundas
Hybrid teas, which usually produce single blooms repeatedly over the season, and floribundas, which do the same but in clusters, are both pruned in a fairly similar manner. Both respond well to hard pruning in early spring.

*Prune hybrid tea roses hard to around 15cm (6in) high.*

*Floribundas are left a little taller, at least 20cm (8in) from the ground.*

* First remove any dead, diseased, damaged growth completely.
* Remove any weak and crossing stems, and any growing inwards.
* Identify the oldest stems and prune some or all back to the ground leaving 3–5 of the strongest, youngest stems to provide next year's framework for hybrid teas and 6–8 for floribundas.
* Cut back the remaining stems of hybrid teas to around 15cm (6in), which is roughly the length of a pair of secateurs. Where possible make a sloping cut just above an outward-facing bud. If you cannot find one, cut at the right height and check again after new shoots have formed and remove any stubs that have died back. Cut floribundas a little higher, around 20–30cm (8–12in) from the ground.
* During summer deadhead regularly to prevent your roses from setting seed. Either bend the stem and snap off the head, or cut back with secateurs to a strong bud lower down. The latter will promote more flower buds but they will take longer to develop than snapping off does.
* In windy areas removing tall growth by a third in autumn may help prevent wind rock loosening the roots.

**Species roses**

Species roses, and old roses that only flower once, can be pruned in winter or early spring like other flowering shrubs. Deadheading is unnecessary and prevents decorative rosehips from forming, so it is best to leave pruning until spring to give birds a chance to feast.

In early spring remove dead and diseased material and cut back stems by about a third to keep it within bounds. Occasionally remove a couple of older stems right back to the ground to encourage new, stronger shoots to form. Cut out any weak and crossing branches to leave a good, open framework.

Modern shrub roses have been bred with all the tough characteristics of these older roses but with extra ability to repeat flower. Normally they can be treated in the same way.

All of the above can be trimmed with a hedge trimmer in early spring, if wished.

## Climbing and rambling roses

Both climbing and rambling roses are pruned in autumn purely for ease. It is much easier to manipulate and tie in the long stems when they are still green and pliable. Over winter they will begin to harden and become more woody, making it much more difficult to attach them to their supports, whether this be a pillar or wire.

Both are pruned in a similar manner and the main difference between them is, in most cases, their flowering pattern. Ramblers flower once, climbers tend to be repeat-flowering, although there are grey areas in between.

*Pruning a climbing rose.*

**Pruning a climbing rose**

* It is usually necessary to remove some, if not all, of the previous ties before pruning and to carefully unwind any pillar roses from their support.
* First cut out any dead and diseased growth and weak branches.
* Remove one in three of the older stems right back to ground level, if possible, leaving enough stems to provide good coverage for the support in the future. Do not remove any new growth coming from the base.
* Reduce all the sideshoots on the remaining main stems back to two or three healthy buds all the way along their length. There is no need to reduce the length of the main stems unless absolutely necessary. On the whole it's better to cut out the longest stems completely to reduce the height.
* Tie the remaining stems back into their supports. On walls, reattach in a fan shape, trying to cover as much space as possible and to keep branches more horizontal than vertical since this promotes better flowering. On pillars or other vertical supports, wind the stems around in both directions for the best coverage, tying in where necessary.

# PRUNING CLEMATIS

Clematis can offer glorious blooms and interesting seedheads almost throughout the year. This means, however, that pruning clematis can be a slightly tricky business, as different varieties behave in different ways.

To make the gardener's life a little easier, clematis are usually split into three distinct groups, each one treated a little differently. The problem occurs mostly with determining which of the groups the clematis growing in your garden belong to. Ideally it should be mentioned on the label when you bought it. Failing that, if you know the name it is easy enough to look it up. As a last resort, watch carefully and make a note of when your clematis flowers and what kind of wood it flowers on, whether new growth or older. With a little bit of detective work you should be able to sort it out.

All clematis will flourish better if pruned immediately after planting. Reducing their stems by half will encourage plenty of growth and better roots.

## Group 1 clematis
These are fairly easy to identify as this group flower early in spring on the previous year's growth. The group includes climbers such as *Clematis armandii* and *Clematis montana*. They tend to be vigorous, even rampant, and produce copious quantities of small, starry clematis flowers

They usually need little more than a light trim after flowering just to keep them tidy. If vigour is a problem prune any leggy new growth back to a healthy pair of buds or, as a last resort, prune stems back hard to around 15cm (6in) from the ground, being aware that the plant may occasionally not recover from such harsh treatment.

## Group 2 clematis

Group 2 clematis are those with large, showy flowers that flower in early summer on the previous season's growth. Hard pruning would remove this growth and therefore future flowers, so these kinds of clematis are pruned carefully and lightly in spring when it is easy to see where the growth is as the buds start to break.

Remove any dead or diseased wood and any damaged stems, before pruning back from the top of the plant. Prune each stem back to the first pair of healthy buds. Clematis stems are quite brittle for climbers, so be careful not to break them and reduce the flowering potential.

Some Group 2 clematis will produce a second round of flowers later in summer, but that does not mean they should be treated like those in Group 3.

## Group 3 clematis

The main connection between this rather varied group of clematis is their flowering season, from mid- to late summer onwards. Most are small-flowered, although there are some larger-flowered hybrids included in this category. They all flower on the current season's growth, however, so can be hard pruned in spring.

For large, vigorous Group 3 clematis, prune back hard to around 15cm (6in) from the ground, cutting just above a pair of healthy buds in early spring. Less robust plants can be more lightly pruned, removing sideshoots only to encourage new growth, but they too will take harder pruning if required.

# TRAINED FRUIT TREES

Fruit trees are extremely versatile and can be trained into a variety of different shapes. Some of the more popular ones are listed below, but there are far more elaborate shapes that can be created with a bit of imagination and confidence. The advantage of training fruit trees is that not only do they look beautiful, sometimes like works of art, but it also means they can be fitted into the tiniest of spaces.

*Fruit trees can be trained into cordons.*

*A single cordon in its first year.*

*A single cordon in its second year.*

## Oblique cordons

Oblique cordons are suitable for apples and pears on dwarfing rootstocks. Plums can sometimes be trained as cordons, though many are too vigorous. It consists of training a trunk at a 45° angle to slow up the growth and vigour of the tree and getting a better distribution of fruit all along its length. These are suitable for growing against a wall or fence, or trained on a system of wires and posts. The biggest benefit of this system is that it is possible to have lots of different varieties in a small space, as they can be planted at only 45cm (18in) apart. Prune new growth back to two buds in late summer.

Gooseberries and redcurrants can also be trained as upright cordons. Prune new growth back to two buds in winter.

## Stepovers

Suitable for apples on dwarfing rootstocks. Pears and other top fruit tend to be too vigorous. This is an attractive method of edging a vegetable garden or allotment, so called because the trees are so low that they can be 'stepped over'. Similar to a single-tiered espalier, trees need to be supported with posts and a horizontal wire 45cm (18in) above the ground. Prune new growth back to two buds in late summer.

Redcurrants and gooseberries can also be trained as stepovers. Just be careful when stepping over a thorny gooseberry.

## Espalier

One of the most ornate methods of training a fruit tree, espaliers are suitable for apple and pear trees. Chose spur-bearing varieties though, as tip-bearers will end up losing their fruit every time they are pruned back to retain their shape. The system involves training a series of horizontal tiers of branches from a central trunk along wires. Sometimes espaliers can be as high as eight

*A mature espalier-trained apple tree.*

tiers if a suitably vigorous rootstock is chosen. Leave about 25cm (10in) between each tier. Prune new growth back to two buds in late summer on established trees.

Gooseberries and redcurrants can be trained as a two-tier espalier.

## Fan

Fans are probably the most popular method of training fruit trees in a garden, as so many different types are suited to this shape including apples, pears, plums, nectarines, peaches, almonds, cherries (both sour and sweet) and figs. As the name suggests, branches are fanned out, usually against a south-facing wall or fence with growth being tied onto a system of horizontal wires.

Gooseberries and redcurrants are also suitable for fan training.

# PLEACHING

Pleaching is a specialised form of training and shaping on a grand scale. Popular from late medieval times, these raised living walls provide shade and privacy for those walking among them with the security of being at least partially visible. In the past they allowed ladies and gentlemen the chance to meet while retaining

*Pleached trees on their framework.*

a sense of propriety. Today they are increasingly popular as classy additions to formal gardens, providing a precise sense of structure without completely blocking the view as a standard hedge would do.

Rows of trees, usually hornbeam or lime, are planted in lines, then carefully pruned and encouraged to intertwine horizontally, to create a sort of natural screen suspended above a symmetrical line of trunks.

* In the initial stages a framework of wood or wire is needed to ensure the young trees are shaped properly.
* Plant trees that are three or four years old, tall enough to reach the frame, and begin to tie in laterals along the horizontal batons.
* Remove any laterals beneath the bottom baton and any that cannot be tied in above.
* In subsequent years keep tying in sideshoots and train the leader horizontally when it reaches the top of the frame. Remove any badly placed, awkward growth and prune smaller shoots back to one or two buds to encourage bushy growth in the right direction. Gradually a box shape should be built up, with no gaps, and at this point the framework can be dismantled and the top growth trimmed into a clean box shape.

# TOPIARY

Topiary is a form of garden art that has brought out the creative side of gardeners since Roman times, and an area where the most extraordinary flights of fancy have delighted passers-by and visitors over time. From architectural and geometric shapes to animals and chess pieces, topiary is always a bold design statement, although not everyone appreciates the tendency towards whimsicality.

*Creating a simple cone shape.*

Smaller topiary, however, is an excellent way of giving a garden a sense of focus, adding more formality and structural form. Even in informal gardens, topiary makes an excellent foil for the looser, unstructured elements.

Small-leaved plants like box, privet and *Lonicera nitida* work best on a modest scale, although yew, holly and ivy are also common. Yew is normally the plant of choice for big topiary displays.

Specialist topiary shears are available, which are useful for complicated shapes, as are long-handled shears. Larger shapes can be trimmed with a hedge trimmer.

To create your own topiary shape buy healthy, dense specimens of your chosen plant, selecting those with a natural shape that best fits your purpose: a long leader for creating a cone; a more branched, bushy plant for creating a ball.

For fancier shapes, such as a peacock, buy a ready-made frame or create your own using chicken wire and canes.

### Making a simple cone shape

* After planting, trim by eye into the rough shape you want.
* In the second year use canes and wire to make a skeleton of the eventual size and shape to fit over your plant. Continue to cut to shape until eventually it fills the skeleton completely.
* Thereafter, clip regularly to maintain a crisp, geometric look. Take time to clip, working down from the top of the plant to the bottom and removing a little at a time to avoid mistakes that may take a while to correct.

# QUIRKY PRUNING

Topiary and pleaching, espaliers and fans, coppicing and pollarding are all classic forms of training and controlling plants. There is no reason, though, why the techniques involved cannot be applied in infinitely more imaginative ways.

Modern artists, architects and designers are increasingly using living plants to produce individualistic and quirky products and features. Houses incorporating living trees, bridges woven from living rope, sculptures and sculptural effects created by controlling and pruning living wood can be found all over the world. New businesses are even springing up that grow furniture, deliberately shaping living materials into useful items such as chairs, tables and even lampshades that are then 'harvested', a technique that is far more environmentally sound than cutting down whole trees for their wood.

Some of the most popular of these new 'living design' elements are cloud-pruned shrubs and trees, based on traditional bonsai shaping. To achieve this cloud effect, all minor growth from the trunk and branches is cut away to leave only the denser ends of the branches. These are then trimmed gradually into spheres and lozenges, although it may take a couple of years to get the right effect of clouds perching on top of bare branches.

Cleaning up trunks, leaving only a high canopy and some artful, structurally good-looking trunk sculpture is also another design trick that is much quicker to achieve.

With a bit of imaginative flair, a sharp pair of secateurs and a bit of patience there is no limit to what can be achieved in your garden.

*Cloud-pruned trees make a strong design statement.*

# INDEX